This book is dedicated to my children - Mikey, Kobe, and Jojo.

Copyright © 2024 Grow Grit Press LLC. All rights reserved. No part of this book may be reproduced in any form without permission in writing from the publisher. Please send bulk order requests to info@ninjalifehacks.tv

Paperback ISBN: 978-1-63731-904-8
Hardcover ISBN: 978-1-63731-906-2
eBook ISBN: 978-1-63731-905-5

Printed and bound in the USA.
NinjaLifeHacks.tv

by Mary Nhin

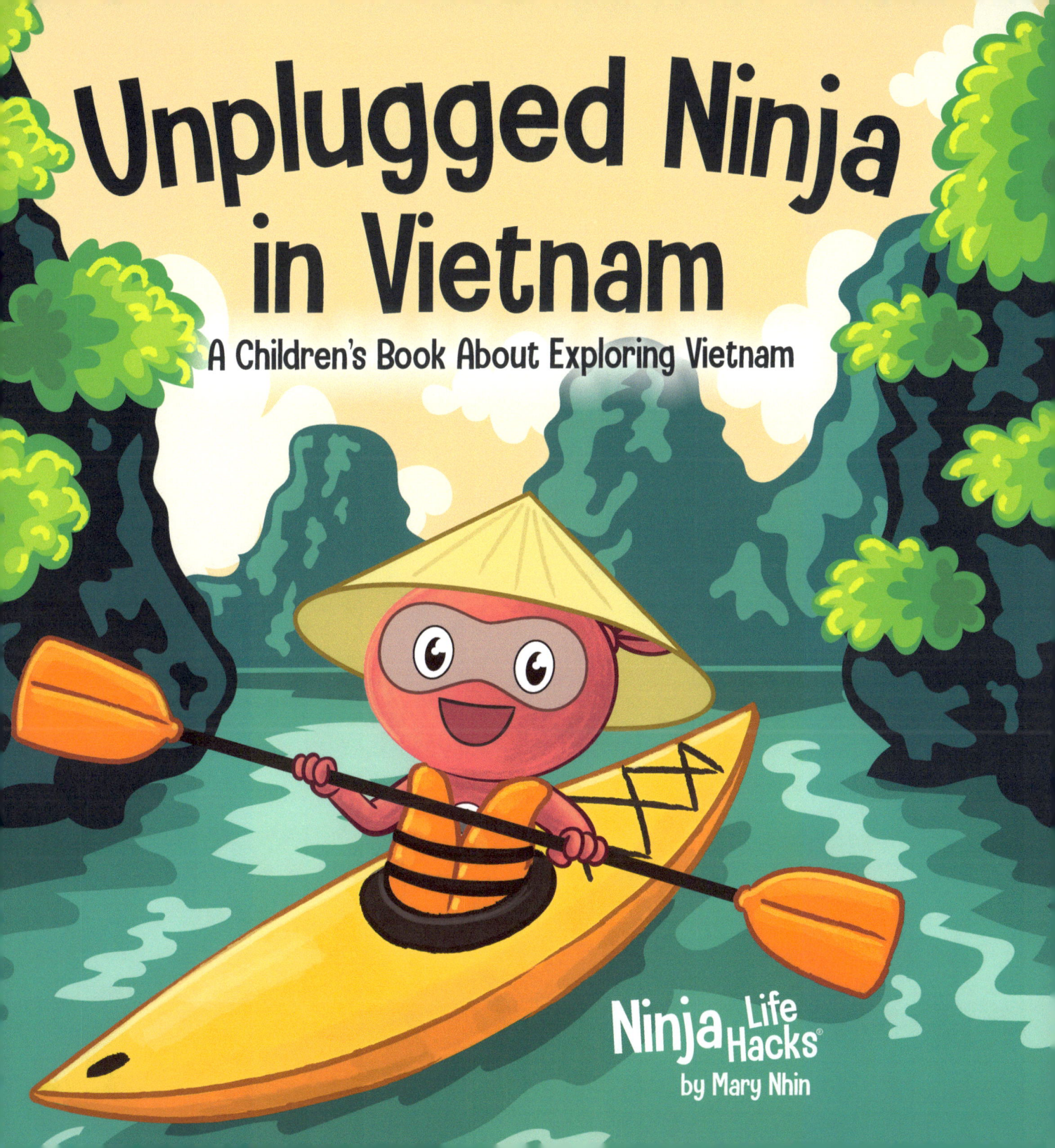

At first, I pouted, "No games? No fun?"
But then she smiled, "An adventure has begun!"
So off we went, on a big airplane,
Where Mom said I'd have less eye strain.

We landed first in Sapa's green hills,
The mountains there gave me big thrills.
We hiked through fields, so bright and wide,
No screens in sight, just countryside.

Next stop was Ninh Binh's caves so deep,
In darkened halls, we'd quietly creep.
Through winding paths and rivers wide,
My mind **reset** with the mysteries inside.

Vietnam's beautiful landscape was so green,
We biked through beauty I'd never seen.
Past rivers wide and tall bamboo,
The rice fields were fresh and new.

Then off to Hoi An, oh what a delight,
Where lanterns glow in the soft night light.
The river shimmered with lanterns afloat,
Reconnecting with nature in a dreamboat.

Next, we hopped in a round basket boat,
I hoped it would keep us all afloat.
Through palm-lined rivers, we felt so free,
The magic of Hoi An surrounding me.

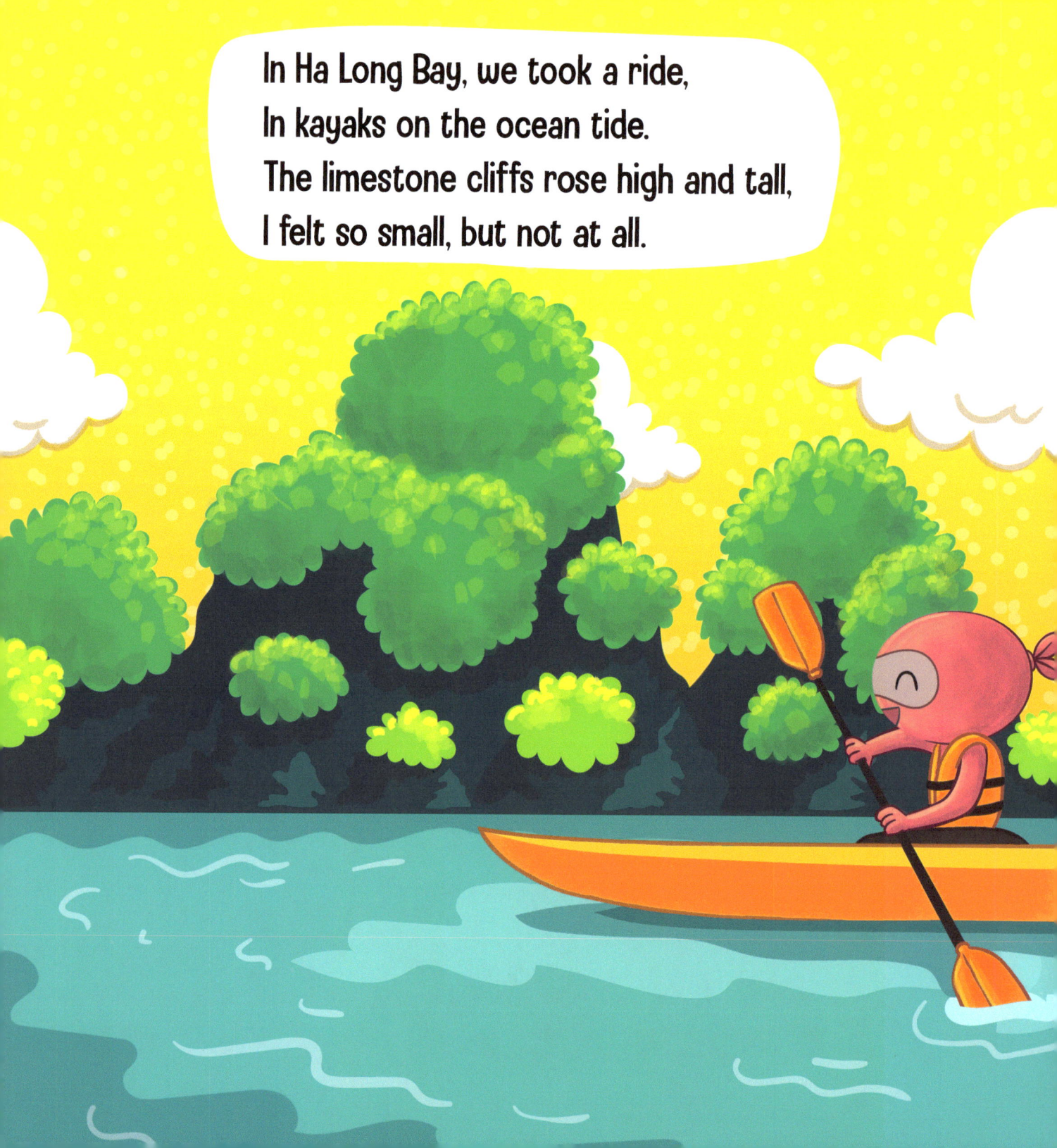

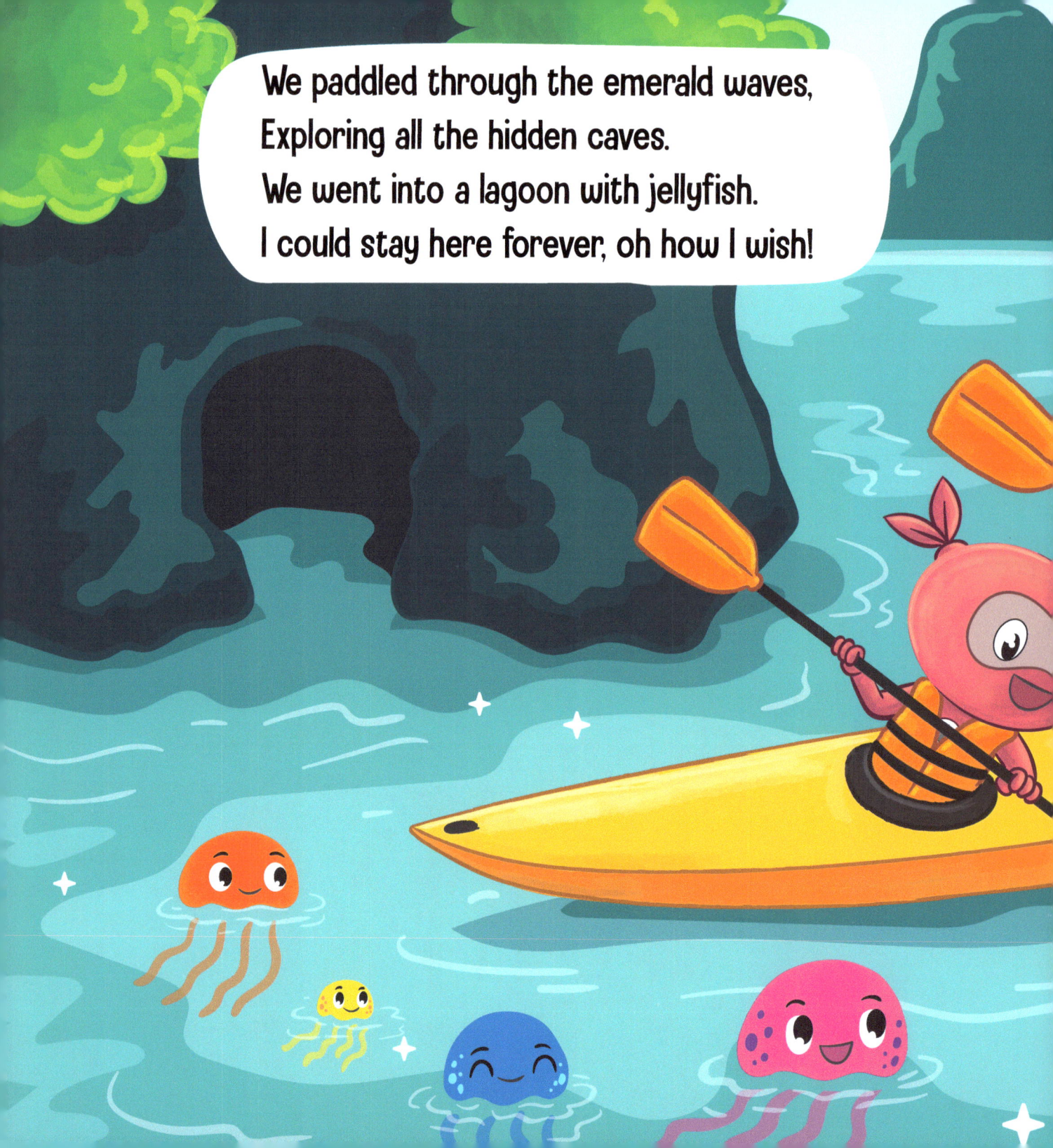

We paddled through the emerald waves,
Exploring all the hidden caves.
We went into a lagoon with jellyfish.
I could stay here forever, oh how I wish!

The screen at home was now far behind,
A world of wonder I did find.
Vietnam's beauty was so vast and grand,
A place to roam while we held hands.

Me and Jojo reaching the Mua Cave viewpoint

Biking in Ninh Binh

Hiking in Sapa

Canoeing in Ha Long Bay

Incense farm near Hanoi

Me, Kang, Jojo, and a friend, Michael, in Hoi An

Lanterns in Hoi An